Surviving
HOLLYWOOD

HOW TO ENSURE THE ACTING INDUSTRY DOESN'T CHEW YOU UP AND SPIT YOU OUT

Surviving
HOLLYWOOD

HOW TO ENSURE THE ACTING INDUSTRY DOESN'T CHEW YOU UP AND SPIT YOU OUT

WORKING ACTRESS, JULIA FARINO, PROVIDES VALUABLE TIPS AND ADVICE TO HELP AVOID THE PITFALLS AND STAY THE COURSE

JULIA FARINO

Julia Farino Publishing
www.juliafarino.com

Edited by Karen Gee
Photography by Elina Dmitrieva at ActorsEssentials
Back cover photo by Nora Schäfer
Cover design, typesetting: WorkingType (www.workingtype.com.au)

Disclaimer: The materials in this book are for general information
purposes only and should not be interpreted as legal advice or legal
opinion. Readers should not act or refrain from acting upon this
information without seeking professional advice.

For Mum and Dad

ACKNOWLEDGMENTS

I would like to thank all the people that helped me with the completion of this book.

With special thanks to:

Jacinta Marasco, Martin Wagner, Anjanette Fennell, Karen Gee, Luke Harris, Kara Sullivan, Paula Miller, Kandace Caine, Lisa Gorgin.

Contents

Introduction

t's fair to assume that when people get married, the last thing they are thinking about is divorce. They enter into marriage believing, wholeheartedly, that it will be forever. However, the statistics show that a lot of marriages falter.

When it comes to actors moving to Hollywood, there appears to be a similar scenario. People come here to pursue their dreams with drive and energy but there are many times when it doesn't work out.

In the 2019 survey of actors on the Internet Movie Database (IMDb) carried out by Queen Mary University of London, it was found that 70 per cent of actors have careers that last for only one year. If you've just started out, you'll want to be one of the 30 per cent of actors who make it past a year — and if you've been in the business for longer than a year, congratulations, you're already in the 30 per cent!

I'm a British actor who has worked in the industry for over 30 years, having spent the last eight of them in Hollywood, and a couple of years ago I noticed that most of the people I'd met when I first came to Los Angeles weren't around anymore. It got me thinking. Why was I still here when so many people had left? I'd met plenty of wonderful actors so it wasn't to do with talent.

I came to the conclusion that I am still here because of the way I approach the business side of the industry. So I've decided to share some of my experiences. There are plenty of books on stage craft and camera technique but a lot of people shy away from telling the hard truths about the business. I make no claim that this book will guarantee fame and fortune but I hope that in putting my thoughts together, I might be able to help other actors stay the course or, at least, help them stick around long enough to get that lucky break!

Note:

For the purposes of this book and to avoid clunky writing, I have used the words "actor" and "actors" to apply to both male and female performers. Personally, I don't like using the male term for all performers. I wish there was a gender-neutral word so if you can think of one, please get in touch and we can spread the word!

Chapter 1

Day-to-day survival as an actor

Before we delve into living and working in Hollywood, I'd like to share a few, basic insights that will help you understand the industry — and the role of the actor within it — a little better.

WARNING: these tips might cause distress!

TIP 1:
Talent doesn't necessarily get you the job

I have been cast many times as a mother or daughter because I look like another actor. I have been cast because I am only 5' 2" and a project requires someone petite. I play northern European roles because I have blonde hair and fair skin. I have strong features so I get cast in professional business roles such as lawyers, doctors and CEOs.

Unlike other jobs, your craft and skills can count for very little. What you look like is a huge part of casting. No matter how good an actor you are, the parts you are offered will be restricted by your physicality. Don't fight it, embrace it.

Once you find success, you may have more opportunity to be cast against type but, in general, the way you look will dictate the roles you are offered. I witness this all the time. I work with people who look right for a part but are poor actors. Production, for some reason, is happier to spend time working with these people to get a halfway decent performance out of them than to cast someone slightly outside the casting bracket who actually has talent.

But even if you look the part, there are plenty of other actors who look and can play the part too. Your job is to stand out and the trick is to work out who you are and what sets you apart. What you are actually selling is yourself.

You are unique. No one can play the role like you because no one else is you and once you discover what makes you special, you can trust in the knowledge that you have no competition.

If you get called in to audition and then appear calm and confident in what you have to offer, you are 90 per cent of the way there. If you can turn in a performance on top of this, then you just might get the job.

TIP 2:
Be available for auditions

This sounds like a no-brainer but I meet so many people who treat this career like a hobby not a profession. You need to be in it for the long haul. Other people arrange the rest of their lives around their jobs. You must do the same.

Last-minute auditions happen a lot. If you have a "non-acting" job, it must be flexible. Know that you can get cover at short notice or, if you have kids, that you have someone you can contact to watch your children.

Make sure you are not too exhausted from the "non-acting" job to prepare for an audition and that you have the focus required to audition well when you get in the room.

Whatever your other life commitments, on any given day you have to have the time and energy to get to an audition or to do a self-tape (see Tip 12, p.29) to send to casting. There will be many times when you will only have the evening before to prepare and sometimes you can be called in on the day. In the last two weeks, for example, I've had three auditions that have come in on the day. This is unusual but you have to be prepared for anything to happen as, at some point, it usually does.

TIP 3:
Check your ego

. . . .

Plenty of people with big egos are employed but to ensure a long career, you'll have more successful working relationships if you're prepared to be part of the team. Know the difference between being cocky and having confidence. Passion sells, not arrogance.

Working in film, TV and on stage are all collaborative processes with everyone in the cast, crew and production team working together to create the best end result. Everyone is still an individual and brings their own skills but each person needs to be on the same page to make a project gel, so don't be too wedded to your ideas; be prepared to adapt.

When you build good relationships working on a project, you are likely to generate repeat work and be offered future roles as people will already trust your talent and input. And let's be truthful here: we'd all take a direct offer over having to audition!

TIP 4:
How to bounce back

In the past six months, I have been pinned for six different projects: a feature film, a TV show, a commercial in Europe and three commercials in the US but I have been released from them all.

Being put "on hold", "on avail" or "pinned" for a role means that you are in the mix and down to the last few actors being considered for the part. You are very close to being cast but you still may not get the job, so you have to learn how to deal with the disappointment if it doesn't work out.

There are many reasons why you didn't get the role and most of them you can't control. You might not be cast because you look like the director's ex-partner and there is no way that they want to spend three weeks on set with you reminding them daily of a painful break-up!

The trick when auditioning is not to think about booking the job but to make sure that your work is compelling and memorable, so that if, for all the reasons you can't control, the job doesn't work out for you, you will now be on the radar of the casting director, director and producer for future projects.

Try to see the glass as half full, not half empty. Celebrate that probably hundreds of submissions were received and that you were good enough to get down to the last few. Take yourself out and spoil yourself; give yourself a pat on the back for getting this far. This job didn't work out but, hopefully, it will lead to work further down the line.

Chapter 2

Marketing materials and how to stand out

TIP 5:
Understand how other people see you

Actors are notoriously bad at selecting their own head-shots; it is rarely the photo that their agent or even their friends would choose as the most representative. How we view ourselves is often not the way other people see us.

With this in mind, it can be very useful to do a branding survey. Ask, friends, family, people in the business and people outside the business, the following four questions and then compile the results. You will see a definite casting profile appear.

1. List three character types you think I could play (e.g. bar tender, lawyer, soldier):

   _____

   _____

2. Pick one current comedy TV show and one TV drama you would cast me in:

   _____

   _____

3. Write down three adjectives that describe my personality (e.g. sophisticated, timid, quirky):

   _____

   _____

4. What do think my playing age range is (e.g. 25–35 years old)?

   _____

   _____

Note: In order for the answers to be completely truthful (age is usually the big one here!) it can be useful to ask one of your friends to receive the completed surveys and put together a list of the responses for you so that the answers are a little more anonymous.

Once you have a list of shows and characters, you can keep an eye out for roles suited to your brand and start to contact the casting directors, directors and producers from these shows. I expand more on this in Chapter 5, "The business part of show business".

TIP 6:
Have headshots that reflect your brand

Hard copy headshots are almost a thing of the past — most casting directors will be using online casting platforms. Your photo is the first thing that casting sees and it needs to stand out on a page full of thumbnail size pictures.

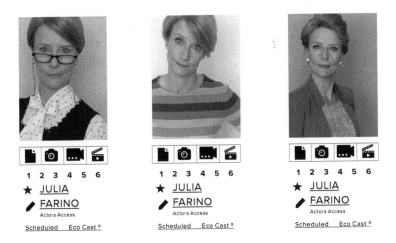

Make sure your headshot looks like you! Maybe not you as you get out of bed in the morning or at your absolute best, all dolled up for a friend's wedding, but you on a good day.

Some photographers offer makeup artists but I always suggest doing your own makeup for your headshots as you will do your own makeup for your auditions. Your photo will be more representative this way.

I don't like touch-ups on photographs but if you want to do this, make sure you don't overdo it. Casting directors will not be impressed if they bring you in for "super hot girl" and you walk into the room looking like the girl next door. There are lots of roles for the girl next door so sell what you are, not what you think they want or what you wish you were.

Search online through other actors' headshots and see which ones jump out at you. The name of the photographer should be listed. If you have friends who are actors and you like their headshots, ask them who they used. You don't need to spend a fortune on a good photographer. Do your research and you will be able to find someone suitable at a reasonable price.

Headshots have trends so keep your headshots up to date. And use a photo that represents who you are now, not a photo that you love that was taken ten years ago!

Remember, your photo should reflect your brand so if you play geeky nerd, don't start with the sexy, bad boy pout when you get to the photo session; you will waste your money!

TIP 7:
Get a demo reel

Having arrived in Los Angeles with mainly theater credits, I decided to employ a demo reel company to write me three 1-minute, quality, original scenes that would pass as clips from a TV show or film:

- a tough detective (drama)

- a cougar-type boss (dramedy)

- a Type A, single mom (comedy)

I used these clips for my demo reel while I built up more footage working on short films and web series.

These types of companies don't come cheap and as casting directors probably won't have time to watch more than 30 seconds of a clip, if you decide to use this type of service, I'd advise you to use a company that offers a speed reel (sizzle reel) package offering 30-second scenes. This will be a lot cheaper.

Casting directors don't like to watch poor quality footage — they will just switch it off. But no footage at all can be a problem. Some of the casting websites in Los Angeles will bump you to the bottom of the list if you don't have a demo reel attached to your submission.

If you don't have on-camera work and you don't wish to use a demo reel company, another option is to record yourself. If you have a bunch of friends, you can find a location and shoot a scene. Entire feature films have been shot on android phones so the quality is good enough but make sure the sound is good too. *Never* shoot a scene from a film or TV show; always use original material. Writers are two a penny in Hollywood so throw a stone and you'll probably hit one who will be happy to write you a scene.

For a temporary solution, if you don't know anyone that can help you shoot a scene, you can have a professional, excellent quality self-tape shot for very little money but you must grab the casting director's attention from the top of the scene in order to keep their interest. I would recommend this only as a stopgap while you work on getting some professional film and television footage together for a proper reel.

And remember, whether you come to Los Angeles with a reel or not, now that you know your casting type, make sure the footage on your reel reflects this.

Chapter 3

Training and auditioning

Some people come to Hollywood well trained in stage as well as camera craft, some come with no training at all, some have one or the other. Whether you are at the beginning of your career or already established, Los Angeles is full of great courses, so do your research and you will find classes that are right for you.

TIP 8:
Do I really need to go to class?

There will always be the rare person who rocks up in Hollywood without any training and lands that lead role in a hit TV show, but in what other profession would you expect to work without any study? You might get lucky once but you will probably very soon encounter a role that requires acting skills you don't have.

There are classes for every level in Hollywood. Do your research, ask around, get recommendations. I took a three-year musical theater diploma and a three-year degree in Sociology and Drama long before I came out to Los Angeles but it is always worth refreshing your skills.

There are plenty of people in Hollywood who will tell you that acting is a muscle and that you need to be in class all the time to keep that muscle flexed. I personally feel the muscle I need to keep flexed is my audition technique so that I can handle my nerves. I try to get myself as many auditions as I can on smaller projects so that I'm audition-ready for the bigger auditions.

If you are comfortable with your acting training when you arrive in Hollywood, there are many other classes worth exploring: audition technique, improvisation, on-camera, comedy, body and movement, singing and voice-over classes are just a few.

Most studios will let you audit a class. This allows you to sit in and watch a class for free so that you can determine whether you think it will be suitable for your needs. You should call ahead and ask if you can audit a class before you attend.

Be warned though — Hollywood has a captive market so prices for courses and coaching are inflated. I recently recorded a new voice-over reel and it was cheaper for me to pay for a flight back to the UK *and* the session fee to record it in London than to pay the going rate in Hollywood! You will need to shop around and compare prices. The best value I have found in Los Angeles are the improvisation courses (I studied at The Groundlings) and I pay a yearly membership fee to Film Independent. This is a group for independent film makers that offers several screenings a month followed by Q&A sessions, holds seminars about the industry and hosts writing, producing and directing labs.

TIP 9:
If you are fresh off the boat,
master an American accent

Do I really need to do an American accent, I hear you ask? The short answer is no, you don't. But if you do master how to lose your accent, it will open up many more opportunities; the more skills you can offer, the better your chances of getting an audition and work.

Your unique selling point is that you are an international actor but being able to lose my British accent has helped get me through the door even if I've eventually booked the job and used my own accent. Looking at the work I have booked since I have been here, it splits roughly down the middle with 50 per cent using my English accent and 50 per cent using an American accent. Without the American accent, I would have worked half as much.

Also, I audition for many commercials and nearly all of these are American products and require an American accent.

When you get an audition, if no accent is specified, decide whether the role could potentially work using your own accent. Go into the room offering what you do best and then offer alternative accents if, and when, it is appropriate.

As a British actress, when I arrived in Los Angeles I was told to lose my accent for an audition unless the role was British. I was advised that it was best to go into the room using my American accent and not to let casting know I was British until I'd finished my audition. The rationale behind this is that, if they know you are British before you read, they will listen out for flaws in your American accent.

I followed this advice for two years and hated every second of it. I could chat to the production team with an American accent but American Julia didn't have English Julia's personality and I always felt like a fraud and as if I was trying to trick them in some way.

After two years of not feeling completely comfortable when I auditioned, I decided to trust that my US accent was good enough for them to scrutinize even if I let them know I was British before reading the scene. Ever since then, I have felt much happier and I can now be myself and relax when I'm in the room.

TIP 10:
Develop your audition technique

First, remember that an audition is not a test; don't worry what anyone else is expecting. Prepare well and remember that, for the time you are in the room, you get to do what you're passionate about.

Your audition technique and how you perform on set/stage are different skills. For an audition, you will generally be reading to someone off-camera (the reader) and without set, props or costume. Occasionally, you may be asked to read with another actor but this is more likely for theater work and rare at film and television auditions.

When you walk into the room, smile — it will put everyone at ease and then you're already off to a good start. If you get nervous, relax; even the great Dame Judi suffers from nerves but she uses them to her advantage.

I'm always fearful. Fear generates in you a huge energy.
You can use it. When I feel that fear mounting, I think,
"Oh yes, there it is!" It's like petrol.
— **Dame Judi Dench**

I'm not going to go into scene study and acting technique here; you can learn these in class or from other books. The following guidelines cover the practical side of auditioning.

Theatrical
(Film, TV and theater) auditions

1. Don't staple the sides (the name used for the pages of the scene or sections of the script you need to audition with). This makes it easier to hold the pages and move through them separately.

2. If you don't know the show, search the internet and watch episodes to give you a feel for the style of the piece. If it's a new project, you can determine the genre from the layout of the sides:

   • Single-camera comedy and TV drama are single spaced.

   • Film is single spaced and usually with more description.

   • Multi-camera comedy scripts are double spaced with the action in capital letters.

   • Daytime drama will be double spaced with little or no action indicated.

3. Use any information on the sides to help you decide where you are in the story:

- The page number will indicate where you are in the timeline.

- The title, stage directions and any crossed out dialogue can help you place the scene and give history and personalities to the characters.

4. Lose any action in the script that isn't necessary. If the action is important to the story, try not to mime; show it another way (e.g. if you can't be at a desk typing, then have a file in your hands that you can be thumbing through instead, or if you are washing up, take a towel that you can be drying your hands on and throw over your shoulder).

5. Don't drop the energy — some readers will give you a performance, some may just say the lines. You may also have to read with an inexperienced actor but don't let it affect the energy of your own performance.

6. Prepare yourself for every eventuality in the room: be prepared to meet one casting director or a whole panel from the production team; prepare for the camera being on either side of the room or in the middle; be ready to audition sitting or standing. Think of anything that could happen in the room that could throw you and work out how you will handle it.

7. Take direction when you're in the room. Don't be too attached to what you have prepared. You must be flexible.

8. Don't wear costumes unless specifically asked to do so.

9. Always rehearse the scene at different speeds. Some casting directors will gallop through the lines and it can be hard to keep up if you've only practised running the scene at one speed.

> I auditioned for the role of Sharon Schieber in the feature film, Gone Girl. The scene was three pages long, around three minutes.
>
> However, when we got in the room, the casting director read so quickly that we got through the pages in less than a minute!
>
> This has happened to me several times at auditions where the reader bangs out the lines at breakneck speed. I've never worked out why casting directors do this: are they checking you are on the ball, seeing how you deal with a fast delivery, wanting to get through the auditions quickly? I just don't know but it is very difficult to keep up unless you have prepared for this.

10. At the end of your audition, don't expect validation. Casting may or may not comment. Either way, it doesn't mean you've done well or badly.

Remember, there are so many other factors that will lead to you either getting or not getting the role so don't be too attached to the outcome. The only thing you can control is the quality of your work in the audition room.

Commercial auditions

1. Research the product or company before you go to the audition and watch other commercials for this brand. Then you can get an idea of the advertising style, so you don't go in with your best comedy routine when they are looking for an earnest, corporate vibe.

2. Sometimes you will be sent sides or a storyboard, but for most commercial auditions you won't know what you need to do before you get to the casting. So go early and find out what is expected of you before you sign in at the audition.

3. A lot of auditions will require you to improvise a scene.

4. If you are sent sides, you will not take these into the room with you. The sides will be written out onto a board for you to refer to when you audition. When you get into the room, ask for some time to read through the text before you audition so you know where to find your place on the board.

5. Buttons — some actors like to add a button to a script to end the scene. This is a short line to add a bit of more of your personality to your audition, but it must work within the overall sense of the piece. If I feel that adding something extra works, I will add three or four words to the end of scene to tie it up nicely. It's the equivalent of the drum/cymbal — ba dum tsssh — that you hear at the end of a joke! And be original. Never use the tagline for the commercial as your button.

6. Again, as with theatrical auditions, don't be too wedded to what you have prepared; be flexible. I've often prepared auditions following the breakdown I have been given but have then been asked to do something completely different in the room. It's frustrating but it happens — a lot!

7. Costumes may be required for commercial auditions. For example, you may be asked to wear a doctor's lab coat or a chef's apron. Twice I have been asked to go in full Victorian dress!

Wardrobe: VICTORIAN ERA ATTIRE. PLEASE WEAR HATS. THE PERIOD LOOK OF THIS SPOT IS IMPORTANT. PLEASE DRESS THE PART.

8. Sales pitches are out of fashion. These days most commercials prefer a more personal delivery as if you are talking to a friend about a product rather than trying to sell something.

9. Personality Slate — Often at commercial castings, you can be asked what I call a "beauty pageant" question. This can be anything from, "If you could meet anyone in history, who would it be?" to "Tell me something you have on your bucket list."

This type of question is designed to keep you talking so that the director can get a sense of your personality. Often, production will watch the auditions later with the sound off so it's less about what you say and more to do with the energy you give out. For commercials, they generally want to see you happy and animated.

My trick to answering such questions is to have a topic I love talking about that puts a smile on my face. They don't want to hear about your acting career — if every actor that walked into the room waffled on about their dream acting job, they'd be bored to tears. Choose something else you are passionate about.

My favorite thing is pizza. Who doesn't love pizza! And here's how I make it work:

- Where would you like to travel in the world? Easy, Italy. They have the best pizza.

- If you ran a company, how would you motivate your employees? Buy them all pizza!

- What do you do for exercise? I don't have my pizza delivered, I cycle to pick it up!

- Do you take vitamins? Well, I try and eat healthily but my one weakness is pizza!

Whatever the question, bring the answer round to your favored topic and then expand upon it. In doing this, you will always be engaged and smiling, not frowning while you try to think of something to say.

TIP 11:
Leave them with something
to remember you by

When I was younger, I was asked to audition for the role of Liesl in a UK national tour of *The Sound of Music*. I'd heard on the grapevine that they had cast a sixteen-year-old for the role but then decided she was a little too young to go on tour for a year so, I knew they were looking for someone older and wiser ... Yes, cheekily, I decided to rewrite the lyrics to *Sixteen Going on Seventeen*, Liesl's song in the show.

For those of you who know the lyrics, this was my re-written version:

I'm not sixteen going on seventeen, I'm really 24
But no one would guess it, you must confess it
I can convince, I'm sure

I'm not sixteen going on seventeen,
innocent as a rose
But drinking and smoking, you must be joking
What do I know of those?

Fully, yes, fully prepared am I
To go on national tour
Not timid, not shy, not scared am I
Of those bright lights which lure

> *You need someone, older and wiser*
> *On whom you can rely*
> *I am someone, older and wiser*
> *Please give me a try*

Sadly, I didn't get the job, but eighteen months later I booked another job with the same musical director. He came over to me on the first day of rehearsals and said that he was so pleased to be finally working with me as he'd never forgotten my audition!

It doesn't have to be this elaborate but there are thousands of people auditioning in Hollywood every day, so each time you are given an opportunity, try to think about how to make yourself stand out. Remember, you are already special and have your unique point of view but what else can you bring?

First of all, be excited, love your character, enjoy the opportunity. Out of hundreds of submissions for this role, you and maybe 30 or so other people have been asked to audition so you are already doing something right.

Throw in something physical for them to remember you by. Where it's appropriate for your character, you could wear an intriguing item of clothing so that they can refer to you as the girl with the yellow scarf or the guy with the jazzy tie.

Don't force it but train yourself to think outside the box and consider how you can set yourself apart.

TIP 12:
Know how to self-tape

> I have set up my own studio in the corner of my apartment. I use an inexpensive pair of 600-watt photographic lights with umbrella reflectors, a camera tripod and my android phone. I also bought a roll of photography backdrop paper which I've hung on one wall; gray or light blue are recommended.

We live in an international market and a lot of work is cast off-tape these days. Self-taping — videoing yourself for audition — is a great tool for an actor to use if they are out of town or auditioning for a project in another state or country.

Here are a few guidelines:

1. The self-tape is of your performance only. Shoot a medium shot from mid chest to the top of your head. Any other characters in the scene will be read by another person, "the reader", off-camera.

2. Always have a good reader. Your reader will stand to the side of the camera to read with you for your eye-line. Make sure that the reader's delivery of the lines isn't louder than your performance. If they are standing nearer to the microphone on the camera or phone, adjust for this. Never send a tape leaving out the lines of the other character. If you can't find someone to read with you at short notice, as a last resort, you can record the other lines yourself.

3. Slate: your slate is a shot of you from mid-chest to the top of your head. State your name and any other information they request. Then include a full length shot of yourself. Don't tilt the camera up and down, pull out for this shot.

4. Always follow the self-taping instructions given to you by casting. Sometimes casting request your slate at the beginning of the tape or at the end, or sometimes they ask for it as a separate file. If they don't stipulate, put your slate at the end; hit them with your amazing performance as soon as they start watching.

5. You can use your smartphone if you don't have a camera.

6. Use a blue or gray background, or a plain background.

7. Shoot the scene in landscape, never in portrait.

8. Have good lighting and sound.

9. Don't use the zoom on the camera.

10. Don't use full costume unless they specifically ask for it.

11. Keep the action simple and props to a minimum.

12. Save the file in the format requested or as a .mov file or an MP4, as these can be edited.

13. You might be asked to upload your self-tape to a casting platform or send it by email. If it is too large to send by email, you can send it using one of the free transfer websites that allow you to send larger files (e.g. Dropbox or WeTransfer).

You can set up your own self-tape studio or there are plenty of inexpensive studios where you can book a slot to shoot your self-tape. The studios will provide a reader and send you a copy of the file for you to submit to casting. Some studios will submit the tape direct to casting for you if you have a deadline.

If there are several days before the deadline, always try to self-tape earlier rather than later as a) other auditions may come in and then you find you have run out of time, and b) you want casting to see you first. If you send your tape in on deadline day, casting may already have seen a tape that they love and you're already out of the running.

Some actors dislike self-taping but it is part of the business now so you need to get used to it. I like having my own studio as I can take my time and be more creative than if I book a slot at a self-tape studio. As I said before, often you have very little notice and time is limited, so another useful thing is that I can self-tape at any time of the day or evening.

Once, I had the option to self-tape or to go to an audition. I chose to self-tape. The role was for a lady sitting naked in a sauna. How can you be naked in the room at an audition? Choosing to self-tape meant that I could film myself in the nude! I just held my sides up to cover my modesty!

Last, never send a self-tape for a role that hasn't been requested by casting. If you see a role you want to audition for but you don't have an audition, call the casting office and ask for permission to tape before sending.

TIP 13:
Is the casting director my friend or foe?

Remember, you are the answer to the casting director's problems. They have brought you in because they believe you are right for the role. They aren't sitting there waiting for you to fail; they want you to do your best as it reflects well on their choice to call you in.

Build relationships with each casting director. Thank them for the opportunity.

I've found that 95 per cent of the time, casting directors are lovely and want to help you as much as they can. Sometimes, a casting director may be a little short with you or there is a stressful atmosphere in the room, but don't let it affect your performance. It makes no sense to believe they are out to get you. It might just be that they are having a bad day. They are human, too.

Finally, remember that the competition is fierce and they have an abundance of people to choose from, so just give them your best performance and make sure they remember you for future projects.

TIP 14:
What to do with one line

Most co-star, supporting roles and day players are just there to keep the story going and support the lead characters, so know your place in the story and keep it simple.

Having said that, you always need to fully prepare for a role however small, even if it is non-speaking. A non-speaking role can have just as much impact as a character with lines. If a character wasn't necessary, it would have been cut.

> Once, I had a line that seemed quite straightforward but when I asked the director for background to the story, it turned out that this line was the crux of the scene.

No part is too small, so if you have questions about your line or your place in the story, ask. Sometimes, especially with television, you are there for a day and have never seen a full script so it's important to clarify.

TIP 15:
How to present yourself at an audition

> When I was auditioning for West End shows in the UK, I had an audition for the musical *The Fix*. I decided to try the "relaxed" approach and it worked. Or so I thought. I got a callback for the show but the casting director asked my agent if I really wanted the job. My trying to appear relaxed, had come across as my not giving a damn!

There's a fine line between coming across as relaxed or appearing uninterested. Relax and have fun but always keep your energy levels up and engage with the people in the room.

Take a hard copy of your headshot and résumé. In general, information is digital now but casting might still ask for a hard copy of your information for their files. Cut your résumé down to 10" x 8" size and staple it to the back of your headshot, facing outwards.

Don't be late. Traffic is notoriously terrible in Los Angeles so it's a poor excuse. Take this into account and leave enough time. But if you are running late because you were held up at another audition, let your agent know so that they can notify the casting office. If you have submitted for the role yourself and cannot attend an audition, be polite enough to let them know. Don't just not show up. If you let the casting director know in advance, they will be able to see someone else in your time slot, but if you don't let them know, they will make a note on your file and probably not invite you in for future auditions.

Don't wear perfume or perfumed oils/lotions. Imagine sitting in a room (usually windowless) with actors coming in and out all day and they are all wearing their favorite perfume or aftershave. First, people's tastes are very different and second, even if they liked every scent that came in the room, the mixture of them all is unlikely to be pleasant. Also, plenty of people have allergies — do you want them to watch your audition, or to sneeze through it!

Shaking hands is a common greeting but again, imagine shaking hands with 50 or so actors over an afternoon. Some people are worried about germs so it's best not to do this. But if a casting director or director offers their hand, by all means, accept and shake hands.

After the audition, don't stay for a chat unless they ask a question. You don't need to hang around; they are busy and will want to move on to the next person.

Chapter 4

Agents and managers

As currently stated on the California Department of Industrial Relations website, dir.ca.gov:

Any person or entity involved in arranging employ-ment for an artist in the entertainment field must get a license to operate as a talent agency.

TIP 16:
Know the difference between agents and managers

My first representative in Hollywood called herself a manager. However, she operated like an agent. She had 150 clients and submitted for work and dealt with the contracts. I didn't complain. Why would I? She was getting me out there and finding me work. But in California, a manager cannot submit for roles or negotiate contracts. A manager's role is to provide guidance.

Once a talent agency is licensed, their agents then have the right to solicit employment for actors and negotiate contracts on their behalf. Managers are unlicensed so should not procure employment or deal with contracts. A manager's function is to "manage" you; to advise and offer guidance to make you as marketable as possible and to help develop your career.

However, like my first manager, there are many managers operating more like agents in Los Angeles who will submit for roles, make introductions and handle contracts so all I can say is that maybe they know they could be open to litigation but they are willing to take the risk.

You will have separate agents for each area within the business: theatrical, voice-over, modeling, commercial etc., but you will only need one manager as they will oversee all aspects of your career.

An agent may have up to 150 clients and very little time to talk to you. A manager should have around ten to 20 clients, as they will be giving each actor more personal attention.

TIP 17:
How to get an agent or manager

One of the biggest mistakes that actors make in their careers is to sign with the first agent who will take them and then they get frustrated when things don't work out. You shouldn't want just any old agent — you want to put together a list of people who are right for you, and who have appropriate contacts.

To do this, research the TV shows and films you feel are most likely to book your casting type (if you carry out the branding survey in Chapter 2, the results will be extremely helpful here).

The best place to find this information is IMDbPro (Internet Movie Database Pro). There is an annual fee to join but it is a great resource for industry contacts and information. I use it all the time to look up production and crew on different projects and get contact details for casting directors, agents and managers. Search each project and make a note of the actors who have been cast in these shows in roles that you could play. Then click through to see who represents them. These agents/managers already have contacts with the shows you are suitable for, so you have a much better chance of getting seen for these projects if you sign with these representatives.

Once you have put together a list of suitable agents/managers, research each person and try to find common interests or talking points that you can use when you approach them.

As with most things in life, it's a lot about who you know.

The best way to contact an agent/manager regarding representation is to have a referral from another person in the industry. Ask around and see if you can find a connection through a friend. If you are taking classes, ask other actors who their reps are and see if any of them are on your list. Find out if your classmate has a good relationship with their agent/manager and how long they have been with them. It's best not to ask an actor to refer you; rather, let them offer to put your name forward.

Alternatively, you can make contact by letter/email or cold calling and now that you've done your research and have your list, you will able to make your letter stand out from the hundreds of letters that other actors are sending. Talk about why you feel the agent/manager is a good match for you and mention any shared interests. They will see that you have selected them specifically and haven't just sent out a blanket letter to every agent/manager you could find an address for.

Before you approach any rep, look up each contact on your list and find out how they prefer to receive submissions. Some agents and managers *only* accept industry referrals and won't accept unsolicited submissions. Some prefer email only or letter only. Some don't like drop-offs.

Always follow up a week or so later to make sure that your submission has been received and if they politely say no to you, you can ask if they are happy for you to contact them again in a few months' time. Everything you do is about building relationships.

TIP 18:
Do I need an agent and a manager?

I have a theatrical agent for Los Angeles and a theatrical agent in Atlanta, a US commercial agent and a theatrical agent in the UK. My UK agent also operates as my manager in the US as she is not licensed in California to work as an agent.

The choice is yours: you can have an agent without a manager, a manager without an agent or both.

Some people find it easier to get a manager first and then the manager may help to find you an agent. However, don't assume a manager will do this for you. You must ask if this is something they are happy to help you with. As a manager shouldn't solicit employment or negotiate contracts, if you are offered work while you only have a manager, your manager should use an entertainment lawyer to handle any paperwork.

Some people like to have a "team". Having more people working for you usually generates more bookings. You can have separate agents to submit you for work in different fields of the business, and then the advice from your manager should help with how you present yourself at auditions, giving you the best chance to get work.

Personally, I feel that managers are useful if you are just starting out as they will help guide you at the beginning of your career. And a manager can also be useful when you start to make a name for yourself, or when you hit the big time, as they can advise on the job opportunities that come your way and help establish and maintain your image.

TIP 19:
Build a good relationship

First and foremost, trust your representatives to do their job. It is unlikely that you will see a job that your agent won't have seen, so don't bug them with emails asking them to pitch you if you see a role you are right for. They will already be doing this.

The best time to contact your agent is if you hear about a role that might not have been put out to all the agents in Los Angeles, or if you see a role that you are right for and you have a relationship with the director, producer or writer on the project and your reps aren't aware of this. Send an email and let them know the details of the project and any relationships you have with the production team.

Then your agent can include this information when they submit or pitch you.

Your agent should be aware of any special skills you have but if a breakdown mentions something obscure that they are unaware of, email them about that too.

Tell your agent and manager when you have meetings with other people in the industry as this will be useful for them to know. They can then make a note on your file.

You will be in contact more often with your manager; they should have more time to talk things through, give advice and discuss ways to build your career. As agents can have up to 150 clients, they don't have the time to chat, so don't call or email and ask what they have submitted you for this week, and only send an email when you have news for them such as when you are in a play or have received an award. Keep all emails short and to the point.

Always let your reps know if you are booked for another job or if you are spending any time out of town on vacation. And then send a reminder email a week before you go and an email when you return.

TIP 20:
How much commission should I expect to pay?

Whether you are paying your agent or your manager, and whether the job is union or non-union, will affect the amount of commission you pay. Some agents and managers will ask for your wages to be paid directly to them; they will then take their commission and forward the remaining payment to you. Some representatives are happy for payments to be made direct to you and trust that you will then forward their commission on to them.

Agents

An agency is licensed so an agent can take no more than 10 per cent commission on union work. Salary for time worked is commissionable. Payments for penalties and reimbursements (e.g. missed meal penalties and living expenses) are not commissionable.

If your agent is handling non-union work for you, they may charge you a higher amount of commission as this work is unregulated. They could charge 10 per cent, 15 per cent or 20 per cent. It's up to you what you agree with your agent if you work on non-union projects.

Managers

As managers are unlicensed and unregulated, they can charge more than 10 per cent commission on all work, union and non-union. A decent manager will stick to 10 per cent commission but some will charge 15 per cent or even 20 per cent, so make sure you clarify before you agree to representation.

Remember, if you have a manager and an agent, you will pay commission to both. Your manager will take commission on all your earnings, including: theater, film, TV, modeling, voice-over, commercial, public appearances, etc. Each agent will take commission on salary earned in the field in which they represent you.

TIP 21:
Signing with an agent or manager

I was offered a two-year contract with a manager when I first arrived in Los Angeles, with a month's notice to leave at the end of two years. I considered that two years was too long to commit to representation. I personally wouldn't want to sign for more than a year, and then you can extend if it's working out for both parties.

Things to be aware of:

- *No talent agency shall collect a registration fee.*

- *No talent agency may refer an artist to any person, firm, or corporation in which the talent agency has a direct or indirect financial interest.*

  agentassociation.com

You should never be asked to pay an advance fee for representation. The only money you should pass on to an agent is commission on salary. And you should never be pressured to pay for any services provided by an agency (e.g. headshots taken by the agency's own photographer or classes that are run by the agency).

Before you sign with an agent or manager, ask whether they are happy for you to submit yourself for jobs (self-submit). And whether they expect to take commission on work that you get yourself. Both my commercial agent and my theatrical agent allow me to work on other projects and don't take commission, but I think this is probably the exception rather than the rule.

I currently have a commercial agent and a theatrical agent and haven't signed a contract with either of them. Most reps realize that if it's not working for them, then it's not working for the actor either so there's no point in keeping someone on the books until the end of a contract. It's better to part company. Again, this is probably the exception rather than the rule.

Agents can be cutthroat — don't take it personally. If it doesn't work out with one agent, that doesn't mean it won't work out with another. An email/letter to move on is acceptable from either party. Be respectful and thank your agent if they decide to let you go or if you decide to leave. Be polite and courteous and wish them well going forward.

TIP 22:
Can I have an agent in several states and/or countries?

Most agents are location based so there will be different agents for Los Angeles, New York, Chicago, Atlanta, etc. Some agencies are larger and have offices in a variety of locations so they may be happy to represent you in more than one place.

If you have an agent in Los Angeles, they will be able to submit you for work domestically and internationally but many productions can't afford to fly an actor to their set and pay for accommodation while they are shooting, so they will use talent that lives locally. This is called "local hire".

If you wish to work as a local hire in another region, you should have a base in the area. You need to have an address where you can stay and where production are able to mail your wage checks and you will have to cover any travel expenses to get yourself there as these will not be paid by production.

You can have agents overseas but you need to make sure that all your representatives are happy with your arrangements and you should clarify who will receive commission. It may be that a job is released in the US and elsewhere in the world and that both your US agent and your international agent have submitted you. They may agree to split the commission in this situation but always clarify.

If you have a manager, they will be involved in all projects wherever you work in the world and will expect commission on payments received for both domestic and international work.

TIP 23:
Can I submit for work myself?

Even though I have a team of people representing me, after eight years in Hollywood, I still work to maintain the relationships I have built up within the industry and develop new ones.

I will contact casting directors, directors, writers and producers, if I see or hear about a role I think I am right for and I now don't always have to audition; I am offered work direct — hurrah!

I believe it is an actor's responsibility to look for work as well as their representatives'. There are several online casting platforms where you can sign up and you will be notified when suitable roles are posted. Then you can self-submit.

The main online casting platforms are Actors Access, which is part of Breakdown Services (BDS), and LA Casting, which is part of the Casting Networks group that operates in the rest of the US, Canada, Australia and the UK. There is also Backstage, Now Casting and Casting Frontier and several other platforms that have set up and closed in the time since I have been out here, so it's an ever-charging market.

Self-submitting helps you to build up a network of contacts that will lead to future work so keep a database of who you meet and work with.

When adding your media to your profile on a casting platform, break your reel into 30-second clips so that you can attach relevant clips to each submission. For example, I have:

- tough cop
- overbearing boss
- controlling aunt
- schizophrenic woman
- neurotic mom

When making a submission, there is usually a box where you can add a note to the casting office. Always add a comment. Include information about yourself and why you are suitable for the role and highlight an area of the project that resonates with you. If you know the casting director then send a personal note. Casting directors are human and like to be remembered just like anyone else does.

Chapter 5

The business part of show business

I decided to make the move to Hollywood in February 2011 and came out in November that year. Between February and November, I applied for a work visa, I took accent classes to improve my American accent and booked myself on a networking course so that my first week out here was spent meeting directors, casting directors, writers, producers, agents and managers. This networking week gave me a great foundation and overview as to how the industry worked.

The information in this chapter relating to taxes, work regulations and official documents is based on my own experience and research. However, it is your responsibility to do your own research, contact the relevant professionals and authorities and ensure that you are personally satisfied you meet all your legal and fiscal requirements.

TIP 24:
Six months isn't long enough

I came to Hollywood with a three-year work visa. During this time, I worked in commercials, theater, voice-over, TV and film but only after three years did all my networking, auditioning and studying start to result in regular bookings and offers of repeat work.

Some people may get lucky and arrive in Hollywood and get that break but this book is about survival. If you want to come and give Hollywood "a try" then come for a few months but if you are serious about making a life out here for yourself, then plan for at least a three-year stay.

The business changes all the time, especially with the rise of on-demand streaming platforms and the internet, so even after eight years I am still learning and having to adapt to new business structures within the industry.

TIP 25:
Stage versus film/TV work in Hollywood

Los Angeles is not a theater city. My experiences working in theater here have been poor and most theater productions that I have seen have been lacking. Hollywood is the oldest and highest grossing film industry in the world so it's the place to be for film and TV work. My advice would be that if you want to work in theater, go to New York or London.

However, theater is a good place to be seen, so if you would like to invite casting directors, agents and other industry people to see you in a production, make sure you work with a reputable theater company.

The Center Theatre Group, the Geffen Playhouse and the Pasadena Playhouse are all well respected and have open auditions during the year. The South Coast Repertory also has a very good reputation and casts on a show-by-show basis but it won't be easy to get a job at any of these theaters so another option is to produce your own show. There are plenty of small theaters you can hire and there are theater festivals throughout the year, the Hollywood Fringe Festival being the largest.

TIP 26:
Get stuck into your marketing

As I've already said, it's up to you to work as hard as your agent.

Research shows, producers, directors, casting directors and writers. Look up projects that are right for your casting type and try to connect with the people working on these productions.

Read industry press — keep up with new projects that are being talked about and you may be able to approach a producer or director if you think you are perfect for a role before a casting breakdown is released to all the agents in Hollywood and everyone is in the mix.

Network at film festivals and networking events for industry professionals rather than networking events for actors. Meeting other actors is fun and some actors also write and produce but there will be fewer opportunities to be found at events for actors; you want to hang out with everyone else in the business.

Remember to keep a database of the people you meet and stay in touch with these contacts. Send regular mailouts by postcard and/or email to make sure they keep you in mind when they cast new projects. Casting directors move about all the time and can change address from show to show, so for a current, updated list of casting directors and the shows they are working on, I use castingabout.com

Know stuff other actors don't.

It's about relationships, not jobs, and it's about quality not quantity. You don't need hundreds of good contacts for things to take off; you only need a handful.

Social media

I worked on a TV web show called *Boss Cheer* and the lead roles were played by social media influencers. At the time of shooting, Tessa Brooks had 7.5 million followers and Tristan Tales had 1.5 million followers.

The reason Justin Bieber was booked to be on an episode of *CSI* was because he has over 100 million followers — even if only a tenth of them watched the show it would make the advertisers very happy!

There is a lot of talk at the moment that you won't get booked if you don't have a social media following. I would take this with a pinch of salt. There are a few roles that will be given to social media influencers but this is still a small number.

If you have a large following on social media it can be very useful and you might book a job if the choice is between you and another actor who doesn't have a lot of followers, but spending time and energy on social media trying to add a few hundred people to your accounts won't make much difference. Even paying to build up a following might only result in your adding a few thousand followers.

Unless uploading content onto platforms such as YouTube is your thing, your best use of social media is to network. You can follow casting directors, writers, directors, producers and build up relationships. But this won't happen overnight; slow and steady will win the race.

TIP 27:
Be able to answer to the question, "Tell me about yourself"

When you engage with people, whether at a meeting with an agent or networking at an industry event, don't freeze when someone asks you about yourself.

Never say that you haven't been working much this year and, as all-consuming as this profession can be, remember that you are person as well as an actor so don't just talk about acting. People love to hear stories so have an anecdote to tell; make it personal and something you are passionate about.

It's not the story that is important, it's how it makes your listener feel, so choose an experience that will tug at the heartstrings or make them laugh or both! Whatever you say, you want to make it hard for them to forget you.

TIP 28:
Mix with the best

You never stop learning, so a great way to improve your skills and immerse yourself in the business is to hang out with people who will stretch your talents and improve your overall knowledge of the industry.

Ask people to tell you how they achieved their success — people love to talk about themselves. One way to do this is to find a mentor. Find someone who has had a similar journey to you and is a few steps ahead of you in their career.

You are not contacting a mentor to ask for a job. You want their advice. It will get you out of your comfort zone and help you with blind spots. Do your research before you contact a mentor. Watch their work and find shared interests.

Make it clear that you are not asking for a huge commit-ment; you'd just love to have a coffee and a 20-minute chat. Say how much you would appreciate this.

If you choose someone you don't already know, you might not be able to find their contact details. If this is the case, you can try approaching them through their agent. Call their agent's office, make friends with the receptionist, and ask if it would be possible for them to pass on a letter for you.

Another way to mix with industry professionals is to approach people and ask if they would be happy to be on a panel and share their experiences. You can then invite an audience along to listen and ask questions. And if people are willing to donate their time and share, remember to turn it around and ask if there is anything you can do for them in return.

TIP 29:
Union and non-union work

Union versus non-union work can be a difficult subject to navigate so I will only skim the surface here and offer an overview of the differences. For comprehensive information, visit the union websites listed on p.61.

There is a lot of non-union work in Los Angeles and anyone can work on these projects, so if you're starting out, this is a great way to build up your skills and footage for your demo reel. Non-union projects are unregulated and pay is, in most cases, at a lower rate than on union jobs.

As fees and conditions can vary greatly, thoroughly check each contract and negotiate terms.

As for union work, there are two unions for actors. TV and film actors have the Screen Actors' Guild which has merged with the American Federation of Television and Radio Artists to create SAG-AFTRA. And the theater union for actors is the Actors Equity Association, AEA. Both these unions require qualifying criteria in order for an actor to join, and both charge substantial fees upfront and require payment of dues to keep your membership in good standing.

The benefit of being a union member is that wages are good and working conditions have already been negotiated by the union to maintain minimum standards for its members. You also have access to pension and healthcare plans. The bad news is that, once you've joined the union, you can only work on union projects and there are a lot of members fighting for this work. Some actors may resort to taking on non-union jobs but in doing this, they put their membership in jeopardy should the union find out that they have been moonlighting.

Some states have "right to work" legislation allowing union members to work on both union and non-union work but, as stated on FindLaw.com, "In California, right to work laws do not exist." The only way you can work on both union and non-union projects is to elect to become a "financial core" (fi-core) union member. Fi-core is a tricky thing to understand but, as explained on Karmalicity.com, "Very simply, it is a loophole in Federal Labor Law that allows workers to take both Union and non-Union work."

If you become a financial core member of a union, you will no longer enjoy all the rights and benefits of the union. You will not be able to vote or run for office or enjoy the advantages of certain events and workshop programs.

However, putting fi-core to one side, don't assume that if you are not in the union you can't submit on a union project. There are instances where a non-union actor might be the only person a union production wants to cast and they will make an agreement with the union in order for you to join and work on their project. But if you do submit, always make your non-union status clear so that production is aware before you audition.

Also, there are low-budget projects where both union and non-union actors can work together and there are certain non-union projects that might decide they want to cast a union member. If they go down this path, the producer will have to adhere to union rules and regulations for any union talent employed, complete paperwork for them and pay their pension and healthcare contributions.

Like I said; it is pretty complicated!

The general advice is that you should work outside the union on non-union projects until you are experienced enough to compete alongside union actors for work, and then join the union.

For further information and to find out the many ways there are to join the unions, you can visit:

- sagaftra.org

- ActorsEquity.org

TIP 30:
Beware of "pay to play"

There are laws in California to protect actors from being exploited. Under the Krekorian Talent Scam Prevention Act, it is a crime to charge a performer money for the right to audition.

When I arrived in Hollywood, I attended workshop centers where I would pay to have a one-on-one meeting with a casting director. I would perform a scene and be given feedback. One of these sessions took less than 10 minutes and everyone knew that you were really there to get on the casting director's radar and hope that they brought you in for a project they were casting. However, this is considered "pay to play" — paying for the right to audition.

Since I have been in Los Angeles, various casting directors have been prosecuted under "pay to play" laws and most of the casting director workshops I attended when I was first here don't exist any more.

Many of these acting centers have ceased operating but you will still see workshops advertised. Such sessions must state clearly that they are purely educational, offering acting and audition coaching only and are in no way offering work opportunities. Each session should be run as a class not a quick audition of a scene and you're back out the door.

TIP 31:
Federal, state and City of Los Angeles taxes

I took advice when I first moved out to Los Angeles to make sure I filed my taxes correctly. But I later found out I had been given incomplete information, so I went into my local tax office — the Internal Revenue Service (IRS) — to clarify how to file my return. Quite unbelievably, the IRS said they couldn't answer my questions!

It appears that all decisions are left up to the judgment of the professional filing the return, based on what they deem a "reasonable basis" for their decision.

You can use a tax preparer or a CPA (Certified Public Accountant). There are slight differences between a tax preparer and a CPA so find out which one is more suitable for you. My advice would be to ask around and get a recommendation but if you can't get a recommendation, make sure you use a professional that guarantees their work so that if a mistake is made, they will be held responsible, not you.

If you feel you are capable, you can file your return yourself. There are various tax software packages to choose from and the IRS offers free tax software called e-File.

Note: I've found that not all software packages are able to deal with international reporting like foreign tax credits.

You will have to file a federal tax return at the end of the year and a return for every state where you earned money throughout the year. If you've only lived and worked in Los Angeles, you will file a federal return and a California state tax return; but if you worked on a film that shot down in say, Atlanta, you will have to complete a Georgia state tax return at the end of the year as well.

City of Los Angeles tax

No one told me that I needed to register as a business with the City of Los Angeles when I first moved to Hollywood. The City eventually caught up with me and I had to pay three years of back taxes!

The City of Los Angeles charges a business tax. This is completely separate from federal and state taxes. It will only apply if you earn cash income (any income that has not gone through a payroll) within the City for seven or more days a year, as this is considered business income. If you are not sure how to classify your income, check with a professional.

If you do earn cash income, you will need to find your nearest Los Angeles City Office of Finance to register yourself as a small business and get a license. Once you are registered, you will need to complete a form at the beginning of each year to declare your cash income from the previous year, and if your earnings fall beneath their threshold you can apply for an exemption and then no tax will be due.

I found out the hard way that, even if your earnings are under the small business exemption amount, if you haven't declared your income each year and filed for the exemption, taxes will be payable to the City.

TIP 32:
Work visas for international actors

When I first came to the United States, I was granted a visa to work as an "Alien of Extraordinary Ability"!

For any actors coming from overseas, it is essential that you have the necessary working papers as the United States has strict laws regarding employment authorization.

To work in America, the US Citizenship and Immigration Services states that you require one of the following:

- *an employment-related visa which allows you to work for a particular employer*

- *an Employment Authorization Document*

- *a Permanent Resident Card (also known as a Green Card)*

I came out to Los Angeles with a three-year, O1 visa. This is a non-immigrant work visa for an Alien of Extraordinary Ability. This visa allowed me to work in the US but only in the field of entertainment as an actor. In entertainment, O1 visas can be granted to directors, models, writers, producers etc. But you can't have an O1 visa as a director and then work as an actor; you can only work under the description stated on your visa.

I've even heard that a "stage actor" can only work on stage and a "screen actor" can only work in film and television, so make sure you don't put yourself in the wrong category or a limited category. Immigration laws and definitions can change so clarify this with your lawyer before an application is made.

And with this type of visa, you can't get a back-up job in Starbucks or shaking cocktails in a bar; you are authorized to work only in your area of expertise.

In light of this, many studios have found themselves in hot water having thought they'd hired an actor but found out that their "actor" has a visa to work as a "model" so isn't fit for purpose, leading to delays in shooting while they recast. Sadly, this has resulted in a lot of the studios choosing to avoid hiring anyone with this type of visa. It's not fair but it is a reality and worth considering when you apply for work authorization.

That said, I myself worked for five years quite happily on an O1 visa (I now have a Green Card) so there are plenty of production companies that will employ actors with this type of visa.

Also, it is worth noting that while you can join the TV and film union, SAG-AFTRA, when you have an O1 visa, currently the theater union, AEA, will not allow you to join until you have permanent residency.

Don't, whatever you do, overstay the length of time granted to you on your visa. The penalties are harsh and it will make life very difficult for you if you apply for working papers in the future.

Chapter 6

Stand up for your rights

believe, wholeheartedly, that in standing up for ourselves in the workplace, the greater chance we have of
developing mutual respect and achieving equality.

TIP 33:
Know your rights on set

Whether you are working on a union or non-union contract, know your rights on set.

Union, SAG-AFTRA and AEA contracts are mind-blow-
ingly detailed so it will help if you make yourself aware of
your basic rights before you arrive on set, e.g.:

- overtime rules and pay

- missed meal break penalties

- payments for fittings

- payments for use of own wardrobe

- safety regulations

Your agent will know this stuff but they won't be on set with you and could be difficult to reach on the day so, in advance, contact your union for this information and make sure you have the union contact number with you on set in case you have any problems. If you have an issue on set, first speak to a head of department and if they do not take your worries seriously, contact the union and they will be able to advise you.

Keep a record of your call times and wrap times so that when your payment comes through you can check you have been paid correctly. I take a snap shot of any paperwork that I am asked to complete on set.

Non-union contracts are a little more complicated as you have to know the details agreed for each project. So try to be aware of this information before you shoot. However, overriding anything agreed on your contract are federal and state labor laws. You may have signed a low-budget contract for a day rate of $100 but if you end up working ten hours you have not been paid the state minimum hourly rate (which in 2020 is $12/$13 an hour rising to $15 by 2022/2023).

Schedule for California Minimum Wage rate 2017-2023

Date	Minimum Wage for Employers with 25 Employees or Less	Minimum Wage for Employers with 26 Employees or More
January 1, 2017	$10.00/hour	$10.50/hour
January 1, 2018	$10.50/hour	$11.00/hour
January 1, 2019	$11.00/hour	$12.00/hour
January 1, 2020	$12.00/hour	$13.00/hour
January 1, 2021	$13.00/hour	$14.00/hour
January 1, 2022	$14.00/hour	$15.00/hour
January 1, 2023	$15.00/hour	

Source: Department of Industrial Relations, CA.gov

TIP 34:
Don't put up with bullying behavior

When I was in London's West End working in the musical *Les Misérables*, I called in sick. I was rehearsing in a new cast from 10 am to 5 pm every day *and* performing eight shows a week which was just too exhausting and I came down with flu.

The director wasn't at the rehearsal studios when I called so I had to leave a message. When he arrived, he immediately called me and demanded that I came into rehearsals however sick I was.

Anyone who knows me knows that, first, I am always professional and would never take a day off unless it was absolutely necessary and, second, I don't react well to bullying tactics or power plays.

I didn't go into rehearsals that day and I took the weekend off to try to get myself well enough to cope with another four weeks of rehearsal plus eight shows a week.

I worried all weekend as to whether I still had a job but when I saw the director at rehearsals on the Monday, he asked me how I was. I replied that I was a lot better and that was the end of it. I stayed in the show for another ten months.

Many people fear they could lose their job if they don't comply with their boss's wishes so it's worth knowing that in California retaliation, in any form, by an employer is against the law; a company cannot terminate your contract.

As stated on workplacejustice.com:

An employee's formal or informal complaints to the employer regarding unlawful employment practices (such as discrimination or harassment) is a 'protected activity' under California law.

Any workplace harassment or discrimination should be condemned, and I hope that the more we can support individuals and encourage them to speak up, the less this type of behavior will occur.

For me, respect is the key word in any working environment. Everyone has a job to do and no one person's job is any more or less important.

TIP 35:
Don't tolerate sexual harassment #TimesUp

Contact which is offensive, demands for sexual favors, sexual comments, jokes and innuendo and unwelcome advances are all unacceptable.

Report any harassment to your supervisor and if your supervisor is the perpetrator, then report the harassment to their supervisor.

The production company or employer has a duty to investigate when a complaint is made. Report, on set, to a line producer or someone in the production office. If this doesn't result in a satisfactory outcome, SAG-AFTRA and AEA both have a 24-hour hotline to call.

It is worth knowing that Time's Up (timesupnow.com) has a legal defense fund should a matter not be dealt with satisfactorily and financial aid is required.

Only take meetings at a business address or public place. If you are asked to meet at a private venue, politely ask if you can meet at another location or take your manager with you. If you don't have a manager, take your best friend and just say that they are your manager!

Intimacy on set guidelines: nudity clauses/riders

We are now in an era where productions may employ an intimacy coordinator for scenes that include nudity or sex, and this is the best way to make sure everyone is comfortable with what they are being asked to do. However, whether there is an intimacy coordinator or not, you should always have a nudity clause/rider and be aware of the following points, which I have compiled from the *SAG-AFTRA Basic Agreement* and Film Independent's *Everything You Ever Wanted to Know about Nudity Clauses but Were Too Shy to Ask*:

1. An actor must be notified before an audition if nudity or sex acts are expected in a role.

2. Total nudity shall not be required at auditions or interviews.

3. Any degree of nudity and simulated sex acts required in a script, should be agreed upon by the actor before a contract is signed. This is called a nudity clause or nudity rider.

4. Any nudity must be filmed on a closed set. A closed set allows for a more intimate and comfortable environment for the actors, as only essential crew members are present.

5. A designated robe person must be available on set for in-between takes.

6. Any still photography on set, must have prior written consent.

7. If revisions are made to the action before you film, the producer should contact your representatives so that

the changes can be amended on the nudity rider and signed off before you shoot.

8. Even if there is a simulated sex act but no nudity, it is better to agree upon what is expected of an actor before a contract is signed.

9. If you get cold feet before shooting, you have the right not to shoot the scene but the producer will have the right to use a body double to perform the scene exactly as outlined in the nudity rider.

10. Once the scene has been shot, an actor does not have the right to stop the footage from being used.

TIP 36:
Ask for equal pay

The most famous, and extreme, example of pay disparity was when Kevin Spacey was recast in *All the Money in the World* and the leads, Mark Wahlberg and Michelle Williams, were asked to reshoot some of the scenes with Spacey's replacement, Christopher Plummer.

According to usatoday.com, Michelle Williams received an $80 *per diem*, which totaled less than $1000, whereas Mark Wahlberg was paid $1.5 million for reshooting the scenes.

Pay parity is still a problem. To avoid this, some contracts will have a "favored nations" clause, which means the employer agrees to offer the actor the best terms made available to any other actor.

> *"[Favored nations] is an industry term which means that you are getting equal contractual treatment to others on the project — billing, accommodations, and any other contractual provision."*
> **—SAG-AFTRA**

Always try to establish if your rate of pay is fair and sign with an agent who loves to negotiate and will fight for you.

TIP 37:
Choose the face and body you want

I had been in Los Angeles only eleven days when a manager advised me to have Botox injections for my frown lines.

I've always avoided such treatments and am now cashing in on the older roles that other actresses my age don't want to play! And don't think that that means boring roles; last year I played a 50-year-old German superhero!

You may wish to enhance your looks or grow old gracefully; just make sure the choice is yours and no one else's.

Know the types of shows you want to work in. Different shows require different looks. There are glamorous television shows and there are gritty, independent dramas that want you warts and all!

If you want cosmetic procedures, Los Angeles has everything on offer. Do your research. Get recommendations from other people.

Commercials used to cast the perfect "cookie cutter" look but this isn't so fashionable any more. All types, shapes and sizes are now sought after. Your authenticity is what will get you work.

TIP 38:
Remember your reps work for you

It's easy to forget that your agent works for you. It is your career so always be prepared to listen to advice but then decide what is best for you.

You might be offered a role that you don't feel is right for you. You may not be offered the money you feel is worthy of your time. You may be asked to audition when you have a holiday planned and you are desperate for a break.

Remember, it is your career, and you get the final say no matter who is putting pressure on you.

If you need time off, take it. You are no use to your agent if you're burnt out. It's just as much for their benefit as yours. You won't get work when you're running from one audition to the next feeling pressured and frazzled. Weigh up the pros and cons and take the decision that is right for you both mentally and physically. It will stop you from crashing and help you survive in the long-term.

Chapter 7

How to stay sane

t's hard to sustain the pressure of constantly being on call and maintain your energy for when that last-minute audition comes in.

TIP 39:
Find a good work/life balance

When I first came to Los Angeles, I had a manager who sent me out for everything: TV, plays, film, commercials, charity gigs. I was auditioning constantly and my record currently stands at eleven auditions in five days. I'm not complaining but it is exhausting and you have to be able to manage your time and energy to be able to give your best at each audition.

You are on call 24/7 and have to check your messages and emails constantly. I wake up and check my emails and

I check them before I go to bed in case an audition has come in late.

To relieve this stress, I don't have my phone on all the time, but I do monitor my emails and texts. I know that I would go insane if I had my phone beeping at me all the time and I relax more in the time when my phone is off and am more productive as I'm not being constantly distracted.

Also, I don't believe that it's healthy to keep this up seven days a week. You need downtime. A lot of people give themselves a day off a week and I think this is good advice. Go off and do something else or spend quality time with family and friends. If you go at it full on, you will eventually crash and burn and are likely to need a lot more time to recover and get your fitness and energy levels back.

Find a sport, hobby or charity work that takes you out of the race for a while, and try to have a day off from emails and social media. It's amazing how good you feel after a day free from constantly checking your phone.

Most importantly, you're entitled to a vacation and that doesn't mean your agent contacting you while you're away and asking you to self-tape (well, I might make an exception if Steven Spielberg calls!). A total break from it all will mean you return mentally and physically restored and ready for anything that's thrown at you.

TIP 40:
Treat yourself when you have a win

Unless you have a partner or family member or members in the industry, it can be a lonely business and difficult for other people to understand what you go through on a daily basis. You might be the only person who truly gets it when you have success, so make sure you celebrate your wins!

I don't just celebrate when I get a job, I celebrate when I know I have worked hard and prepared well and have turned in a great audition. That's worth a pat on the back because I've done all I can to book the role. The rest is out of my hands.

Always remind yourself how far you've come and not what you haven't yet achieved. So many people just give up. Be one of the few who doesn't.

Note: There may be days when you have a bad audition but when this happens, don't beat yourself up. Give yourself a break; you're allowed to have an off-day. It's difficult but try to let it go, put it behind you and give yourself some downtime. You can use this break to review your objectives. I find that I start to see things a little clearer and I might adjust my approach, which gives me the incentive I need to keep pushing on.

TIP 41:
Keep yourself mentally and physically fit

Self-motivation is difficult and routine is key. I'm not a morning person so struggle to drag myself out of bed each day. Do your best to get up at the same time and have a structure so that you don't get distracted and wonder where the day went. When auditions come in last minute, and you have early call times on shoot days, it's not always easy, but stick to a routine wherever you can.

Motivation comes from having a plan. How are you going to find work, make contacts, build your career? Being proactive will get you results. Results lead to confidence and with confidence, everything in life always becomes a lot easier.

Exercise releases feel-good brain chemicals and these trigger positivity and a healthier mindset, so if the gym's not your thing, find another activity: hiking, tennis, dancing or just walking round the block will boost your energy levels and keep you motivated.

It's easy to get isolated in this business, so make sure you get out and mix with other people. First, we are social beings; human connection is necessary to stop you going stir-crazy. Second, you never know who you will meet when you're out, especially in a town like Los Angeles where probably half the people in line in the coffee shop work in some capacity in show business!

It's obvious but still worth saying: eat well. Good food will give you energy, bad food will make you lethargic. There are so many factors you can't control that may make you want to give up, so use the things you can control to stay healthy and motivated. And drink plenty of water. It is very easy to get dehydrated in Los Angeles and you can't function at your best when you're dehydrated.

Meditation is a useful tool for quietening the mind and relieving stress and anxiety. Even ten minutes a day can be beneficial.

TIP 42:
Have a good support network

I've always said that if I ever made an Oscar acceptance speech (never say never!) I would thank my family at the beginning of the speech and not right at the end, so I'll practise by thanking them here.

"Thank you, Mum, Dad, Teresa, Maria, Paola, Antonia, Stuart, Gabriel, Annie, Kit and Issy. You are the reason that I am still working in this crazy business. Without your love and support, I would not be able to do what I do."

It's very hard to go it alone. Don't be afraid to ask for help from friends and/or family, but don't just contact people when you need something — you won't keep friends that way!

Make sure you hang out with people who are not in the business, as well as industry people. People outside the business will surprise you with their perspective which, more often than not, will help you keep your feet on the ground. It's always fascinating, and usually a reality check, when you see how people outside the business perceive our lives.

Find people who will support you as much as you support them. Create a group that meets weekly or monthly where you can motivate each other and share experiences. This can be a lifeline when you've had a tough day navigating the industry.

Celebrate other people's achievements. This can be difficult when things aren't going well for you, but success is hard to come by in this business so we need to support each other when times are good as well as when they are bad.

TIP 43:
Give back

. . . .

Find a charity that interests you and volunteer.

> I pick fruit and collect unsold produce at farmers' markets, for the charity Food Forward. The charity prevents food waste by rescuing fresh surplus produce, which is then donated to hunger relief agencies.

It's good to find ways of giving back to your community. It's easy to get caught up in your career, so take a step back from everything.

Many students need to complete service hours for college applications so sometimes charities are overflowing with volunteers in Los Angeles. If you can't find a charity that needs your help, think of ways that you can offer your skills. For example, you can host an event, or if you sing, dance or juggle, maybe you can provide the entertainment at a charity function.

I'm not sure it's completely altruistic, either. We all know that when you help other people, often it makes you feel better too. It's also a great thing to do when you've suffered a knockback in your career. It certainly puts things into perspective.

Chapter 8

Living in Los Angeles

Los Angeles is a bit of a jigsaw puzzle. The sprawling City of Los Angeles stretches all the way north to the Granada Hills, and south down to Long Beach, but it doesn't include some of the main areas that people associate with Los Angeles. Beverly Hills, West Hollywood, Westwood, Santa Monica, Culver City, Burbank and Glendale are all separate cities and each has their own jurisdiction.

TIP 44:
Things you should know

Cost of living

Los Angeles is very expensive. I was living in London before I came to Los Angeles, and London isn't a cheap city by any means, but Los Angeles has overtaken London on the list of the world's most expensive cities.

I had budgeted for rent and the cost of buying furniture and a car, money for taking classes and casting registries, for union fees and marketing materials but the one thing that threw out my budget completely was the price of food, cleaning products and toiletries. Most items can be up to three or four times more expensive than London, and compared to the rest of the United States, food in Los Angeles is significantly more expensive.

Health insurance

For people coming from overseas, you need to be aware that the United States does not provide universal health-care unlike other advanced, industrialized countries. So you need to make sure you have medical insurance.

For those of you coming from other states as well as from overseas, be aware that the state of California has passed a mandate that, according to the Franchise Tax Board (CA.gov), "requires Californians to have qualifying health insurance coverage throughout the year." If you don't have insurance and don't qualify for an exemption, you may have to pay a fine.

But should you be uninsured and have an accident with serious or life-threatening injuries, you won't be turned away at a hospital emergency room. As stated on the website patientadvocate.org: "No matter what your insurance status, hospitals and emergency rooms must provide adequate care if your situation qualifies as an emergency [but] just because you were treated despite being uninsured doesn't mean the visit is free. You will be responsible for the full bill."

A full bill for a hospital stay and emergency treatment is likely to amount to thousands of dollars so take advantage of the healthcare plans that California offers through its online health insurance marketplace. You will find many options and can select one that is right for you. You may also qualify for financial help. It can be a little overwhelming, so if you get stuck, use a California certified agent or a private health insurance broker to help you choose a plan.

The weather

Although the climate here is classed as a Mediterranean climate, it is nothing like the Mediterranean conditions I am used to in Europe. There is much less humidity and it often isn't warm at night. Once the sun goes down, it is much cooler in the evenings. The trick is to wear layers and always have a cardigan or jacket to hand.

And be aware that it doesn't matter whether it is hot or cool outside, establishments do not adjust their air-conditioning whatever the time of year, so it will probably be colder in the cinema than outside at the Hollywood Bowl; you will need to take a blanket to both!

The temperatures can vary tremendously depending on where you live in Los Angeles. In the summer, it can be a lot cooler near the ocean as the mountains block the sea breeze from reaching inland areas. The San Fernando Valley can hit temperatures over 100° F (38° C) but it can be 10–15 degrees cooler on the coast.

The Big One

This is how Los Angelenos talk about the next big earthquake, as there are five major fault lines that run below Los Angeles, which could have a devastating effect on the whole region if they shift.

The last big earthquake in Los Angeles was in 1994 in Northridge, North Los Angeles, of magnitude 6.4. But since I have lived in Los Angeles, there was an earthquake of magnitude 7.1, 150 miles north of Los Angeles in Ridgecrest, so you need to be prepared. Unlike other natural disasters, there is very little time to warn people. You can download an earthquake alert app but it will only give you a warning of 15 to 20 seconds.

Read up in advance on earthquake safety tips — you don't run, you drop and take cover — and put together an earthquake kit: water, food supplies, first aid kit, flash light and sturdy shoes, etc.

Wildfires

With the planet heating up, wildfires are more and more frequent in and around Los Angeles. There used to be a fire season but now a fire can start any time of the year. The fires are usually worse between October and March as the Santa Ana winds blow fiercely through Los Angeles, fanning the flames making fires particularly difficult to contain.

Since I have been here, there have been fires within the City of Los Angeles in Brentwood and Bel Air. Areas surrounding the City and in the Hollywood Hills, where there is dry brush and forests that allow fires to catch and spread more easily, are the most likely areas to be affected.

TIP 45:
Where to live

Both renting and purchasing a home in Los Angeles are expensive so budget accordingly.

Los Angeles is sprawling but try to live centrally as it will be easier to get to auditions and shoot locations. I live in the San Fernando Valley, usually referred to as The Valley. This is north of Santa Monica, Beverly Hills, Hollywood and Central Los Angeles but I find it convenient as there are a lot of studios in The Valley and it is only 20 minutes to get to auditions in Hollywood during the day. Rush hour can be a different story, when a 20-minute journey can easily take over an hour!

Most auditions will be in Hollywood, West Hollywood, Studio City, Sherman Oaks, Central LA and Santa Monica.

Most apartment blocks have a swimming pool, which is wonderful. I love swimming but beware, some pools are the size of a foot bath! And if you are coming from overseas you may be surprised to find that your apartment doesn't have a washing machine. Most apartment complexes have shared, on-site laundry facilities, though more modern apartment blocks are finally starting to put washing machines in each unit.

TIP 46:
Getting around

··

Driving

Most people drive in Los Angeles as public transport runs infrequently compared to cities such as New York, Chicago or London. But bear in mind, Los Angeles is second only to New York as the most expensive city in the US to drive and park, and one of the worst US cities for traffic.

If you bring a vehicle into California, you need to register it with the Department of Motor Vehicles (DMV) and fees become due from the date your residency is established, so register your vehicle as soon as you can to avoid penalties. Under the California Vehicle Code, license plates are required on both the front and back of most cars in California. Visit dmv.ca.gov for further information on registering your car.

You must also have SMOG certification for your car. This is to keep exhaust emissions to a minimum as the air quality in California isn't great. I have a hybrid car and, so far, have not needed a SMOG certificate. However, the DMV still gets its money; it charges me a SMOG abatement fee for the privilege of *not* having to get one!

Parking

Always read the signs for street parking. Parking restrictions will be different for each side of the road and vary throughout the different cities in Los Angeles County.

With parking lots, make sure you read each sign. They may hook you in with a big sign saying that parking is free, but it might only be free for the first hour and then $2 for every 15 minutes after that, which can really add up!

Parking Rates

$2.10 Ea 15 Min.
$12.60 Maximum
10% City Tax Included
Lost Ticket Pays Max.

Hours Of Operation
8:30am - 6:00pm M-F
Closed Sat & Sun

Public transport

There are bus and train services in Los Angeles which run regularly but not that often. In London, I knew which bus route would take me where I wanted to go but in Los Angeles, you might miss one bus, and the next quickest option could be to walk to a different junction and take a completely different route. There are many plans in place to improve the transportation system but at the moment, you should leave plenty of time to get from place to place if you're using public transport.

Bikes and scooters

There are several companies that operate bike and scooter hire. Download the company app and use it to locate a bike or scooter. To start the journey, scan the QR code on the vehicle. Don't ride on sidewalks; use bike lanes where possible and obey traffic regulations. To finish the journey, scan the QR code again and don't just leave the bike or scooter lying on the sidewalk for someone to trip over, set it to one side on its stand.

Walking

Because so many people drive in Los Angeles, drivers aren't looking out for pedestrians so make sure you have been seen before you step out into the road.

Don't cross the road when the "Don't Walk" light is showing — believe it or not, since I've been here there have been news reports that pedestrians have been issued tickets for crossing *before* the "Don't Walk" light comes up when the crosswalk clock is ticking down! The safest thing to do is to only cross at traffic lights when the white "Walk" light is showing.

Whenever you walk in an urban area, don't be surprised to see the sidewalk just disappear. Over the years, the infrastructure has been developed with drivers in mind and not pedestrians, so sometimes the sidewalks run out and the only option is to walk in the road, which can be quite dangerous. The flyovers and streets Downtown can be particularly difficult to navigate as a pedestrian.

Flying

You can fly almost anywhere from Los Angeles. The international airport is LAX and then there are smaller airports: Hollywood Burbank Airport (AKA Bob Hope Airport) and Long Beach Airport for domestic flights.

TIP 47:
Dining out

Le Pain Quotidien is a restaurant chain in London which I love, so I was very happy to see their restaurants when I arrived in Los Angeles. However, when I went to the branch in Studio City, I was completely thrown when I was told that I couldn't have a glass of wine with my lunch.

The restaurant didn't have a liquor license as the quota of liquor licenses in the zone had been reached, so this Le Pain Quotidien had to wait until another restaurant in the area closed down before its liquor license might be approved.

So some restaurants might not have a liquor license, plus you need to be aware that even if a restaurant has a liquor license, it may only have a beer and wine license and not a full license that includes spirits. If you can't live without your pre-dinner G&T or your post-dinner brandy, check the establishment has a full liquor license before you book a table.

California's farms produce over 400 commodities so Los Angeles is a great place for finding fresh, local produce and wonderful places to eat. There are all manner of cuisines to be found and many talented chefs and restaurateurs.

Los Angeles is also renowned for its food trucks; the key here is diversity and fusion.

However, Los Angeles is a TV and film studio city with many people starting work at 6 am/7 am or earlier each day, so people eat early in the evenings. Don't be surprised if you're asked to place last orders for the kitchen at 9 pm and the restaurant starts clearing up around you at 10 pm!

Oh, and it's usual to tip 15 to 20 per cent for service.

TIP 48:
Out and about

Outdoors

There are plenty of things to see and do in Los Angeles and the surrounding areas. The beach and the mountains are within driving distance of each other, so if you're up for it you can surf and ski in the same day!

The Hollywood Hills are great for walking and hiking, with excellent views and scenery. You can find outdoor yoga sessions in the Hills too.

Museums and theaters

Los Angeles has built its reputation as a city of culture with plenty of museums and galleries:

- The Getty Museum and The Getty Villa — art, architecture, gardens

- LACMA (Los Angeles County Museum of Art)

- MOCA (Museum of Contemporary Art)

- The Broad — art museum

- Petersen Automotive Museum

- La Brea Tar Pits and Museum

- Griffith Observatory

- Natural History Museum

- California Science Center

- The Annenberg Space for Photography

- Grammy Museum

- Academy Museum

There is even a Museum of Tolerance and a Museum of Weed!

And there are many theaters, including:

- Hollywood Pantages Theatre

- Center Theatre Group: Ahmanson Theatre, Mark Taper Forum, Kirk Douglas Theatre

- Geffen Playhouse

- Pasadena Playhouse

These are the larger theaters and all offer quality shows. There is also the LA Theatre Works, which presents classic and modern plays in audio theater format, screens the UK's *National Theatre Live* series and has a catalog of over 500 audio plays that you can purchase.

My favorite small theater is the non-profit Fountain Theatre, which consistently delivers excellent productions. It develops new material and reworks established plays aiming to reflect the cultural diversity and concerns of Los Angeles and the nation.

Outdoor theaters include:

- Hollywood Bowl

- The Greek Theatre

- Ford Theatres

TIP 49:
Avoid the crazy

Not long after I came to Hollywood, I heard a musician on the radio talking about his first impressions of Los Angeles after he moved here. His analysis was that Hollywood is the only place where people who are quite obviously mentally unstable are allowed to hold positions of power.

Eccentricity is a huge part of show business and if your eccentricity makes money, people will overlook certain conduct. People who like to be noticed gravitate to Hollywood so don't be surprised if you come up against behavior you've not witnessed before. If it's bizarre but harmless, you can engage or walk away. If it's detrimental, take action and report it.

Never think that you have to put up with any sort of behavior that makes you uncomfortable or distressed, whether in the business or out on the street!

Of course, there are eccentric people everywhere in the world; Hollywood just attracts a few more of them.

TIP 50:
For overseas actors

When I presented my California driver license to visit a friend on a military base in Ventura, I was granted access immediately. A few weeks later when I showed my UK driver license, I was denied entry. I had to turn around and drive home.

Identification card

Whether you drive or not, when you arrive in Los Angeles go to the DMV (Department of Motor Vehicles) and complete a driver license or identification card form. Everything will be so much easier if you can produce a California ID card rather than an overseas passport or foreign ID card.

A California ID card may be required when you buy alcohol and upon entry to clubs and bars, when you make credit card purchases and when you need access to buildings/areas that have security. Another form of identification may be accepted but there is the possibility that you may be turned away or refused a purchase with any other form of ID.

Social security card and number

You will need a social security number to work in the US. There are two ways to obtain this. Either you can apply for your social security card and number when you make the application for your immigration visa before you arrive in the US, or you can visit a social security office when you arrive. If you go into a social security office, you will need to take proof of your identity and the documents showing your work authorization and immigration status.

Credit score

It isn't possible to transfer a credit history from another country to the US, as credit reporting differs in each country. If your bank or credit card company operates in the US, you can contact your provider and ask them whether they can give you a kickstart in the US but most banks won't be able to help.

A credit history may be required when you rent or buy a property or car, when you make a purchase and wish to pay in installments, or if you need to get a loan. You may also need a credit report to get a non-acting job, and without a credit history you will have a blank credit report.

The best way to build up your credit history is to apply for a secured credit card.

A secured credit card is designed to establish and develop your credit rating. You provide a security deposit of say, $500, and then you will have a credit line of $500 to spend. Yes, basically, you are spending your own money! You use the card for purchases and pay off the bill each month. Once you have successfully paid your bill over several months (I did it for a year but some banks require less time), your security deposit will be returned to you and you can start to use your card as a traditional credit card. You have now created a credit history for yourself in the US.

Conclusion

When I worked in the UK, I booked mainly theater jobs. I would rehearse and enjoy performing the show for several weeks or months. It was a joy and stress free! However, the stage productions in Los Angeles have limited runs so there is far less time to savor the work and relax. The same is true when you work in film and television, where you often have little time to prepare, you shoot the project for only a short time and then you're back out there running from one audition to the next. The process is constant, stressful and exhausting.

Even if you work on a television show as a series regular the turnaround can be brutal, with only a few days to shoot each episode. Harder still is daytime drama, which produces one episode per day!

Out of all the areas I have covered in this book, I believe the most important key to sustaining a career in Hollywood is managing your time and giving yourself a break when you need it so that you don't burn out. You need to organize your days so that you can handle the (albeit exhilarating) madness of it all!

But before I finish up, there is one last thing that I want to mention. I have met some extraordinary people in Hollywood who have gone above and beyond when it comes to help and support, but there are many other people in Los Angeles who are fickle. I'm used to job insecurity, handling rejection, being away from loved ones, but what I have really struggled with in Hollywood is dealing with people who are only out for what they can get.

I promised myself that I wouldn't allow other people's behavior to change me and I have managed to remain reliable and courteous. However, having been taken advantage of so many times, I am more wary when I first meet people. Out of all the hardships that I have encountered over my 30 years in the business, this narcissistic behavior has been the only thing that has ever made me question whether my career is worth it. Don't be the person who is all take and no give, and steer clear of people like this. I made a lot of friends early on and didn't recognize this behavior until it was too late, so I share my experiences with you in the hope that being forewarned is forearmed.

I can't quite believe that I've been out here for eight years already. Time has flown. I've learned a lot, had successes and made mistakes. I hope that sharing some of my stories will be helpful to any of you who make the move out here and I wish you the best of luck.

To sign off, I'll leave you with a little bit of fun. I have noticed that there is no such word as "no" in Hollywood as, in general, people don't want to offend in case you turn out to be the next Quentin Tarantino. It's also worth noting that many words and phrases mean something different here, so in light of this I have included a glossary to help you navigate the world of "Hollywood speak".

"Hollywood speak" glossary

Word or phrase	Hollywood Definition
No.	*I'm not sure of a definition — I've yet to hear anyone say it!*
Yes.	Might do if nothing better comes up.
Would love to!	Still only a 50 per cent chance I'll be there.
I'll get back to you.	You'll never hear from me again.
Real people.	Anyone other than an actor or model. *Apparently, we aren't real people.*
Normal people.	Same as above. *Actors aren't considered normal either, though there may be some truth in that!*
Attractive.	Average looking.
Stunning.	Reasonably attractive.
Super hot.	Probably involves quite a lot of cosmetic surgery — both women and men!
Good at improvisation.	A request when someone couldn't be bothered to write a script.

Word or phrase	Hollywood Definition
Good job.	Maybe not that great but we can't tell you what we really think as you might know someone important in the business.
You booked it!	You've got the job — congratulations! However, you now can't work on any of this network's TV shows for the next year.
I don't know what's going to happen but ...	*If your agent is saying this, then they are about to drop you!*
My party starts at 7 pm	I, however, won't be there until 9 pm at the earliest.
Can we car pool?	Can you drive?
Can you give me a ride?	I'm not stupid enough to spend money on my own car. *I didn't make this up, someone actually said this to me!*

Made in the USA
Columbia, SC
29 October 2020